MORE
Alternatives to Worksheets

Written by Catherine Hiatt, Doug Wolven,
Gwen Botka, and Jennifer Richmond

Illustrated by Terri Sopp Rae

Edited by Joellyn Cicciarelli and June Hetzel

Project Director: Elizabeth Strauss

CTP ©1994, Creative Teaching Press, Inc., Cypress, CA 90630

MORE Alternatives to Worksheets is just what every teacher needs—a resource book with hundreds of meaningful and motivating activities that students can work on independently. Now you and your students will never be at a loss for exciting and challenging projects.

A welcome change of pace from worksheets, these activities will raise student involvement to new levels and generate genuine enthusiasm for learning. You will love the imaginative alternatives described in this book and so will your students. These activities . . .

- Are adaptable to any theme

- Increase student involvement and motivation

- Require students to apply skills, not just circle answers and fill in blanks

- Emphasize written and oral expression

- Promote critical thinking

- Allow all students to experience success

- Encourage creative expression

- Require minimal teacher preparation

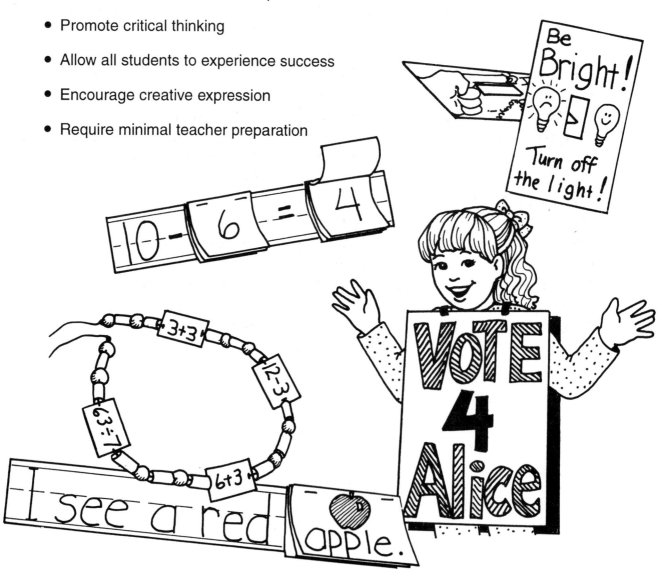

Table of Contents

How to Use This Book

As you look through **MORE Alternatives to Worksheets** you will find many new ideas, along with new twists on old favorites. Choose the project that best suits the needs of your class. The handy list of materials makes teacher preparation easy, and the illustrations help you see at a glance how to complete the project. The patterns you will need are at the back of this book.

Steps to Student Success

 When introducing a new activity to students, you may want them to begin the project as a whole group, then complete it independently. (Kindergarten teachers may find that young students need more direction from an adult.)

 The importance of teacher modeling cannot be overemphasized. When you carefully demonstrate and explain each step your class will know how to proceed in order to complete a successful project. Students are then free to personalize and extend the activity according to their abilities.

 In preparation for the activity, have students brainstorm ideas in a large or small group. Brainstorming lets you find out what students already know about the topic and provides a pool of information that students can draw on as they complete their projects. Mapping, webbing, and making lists and word banks are common ways to brainstorm.

Grouping should be flexible. Students can work individually, with a partner, or in small groups. The activities in this book are especially appropriate for use at learning centers.

 A key element in each activity is a strong emphasis on writing. Younger students can rely on developmental (invented) spelling or dictate their writing ideas. Older students can move toward conventional spelling through the use of dictionaries and editing procedures.

Students learn best when the same concept is presented in several different ways—so use a variety of activities for the same theme topic or concept. Also, don't hesitate to repeat an activity in different subject areas. When students know how to make the project, they can concentrate more on content.

Making it Your Own

Use this book as a resource and as a springboard for ideas. Personalize it by changing the activities to fit the needs of your class, and look for opportunities to apply the new formats to projects you have used in the past. ENJOY!

Bean Cards

Dried beans are useful for a variety of tactile activities. Students have the opportunity to make and practice with textured projects to learn kinesthetically.

Materials:
- a variety of dried beans
- tagboard or cardboard
- glue
- small containers
- pencils, crayons, markers

Directions:
Have students use tagboard or cardboard and glue beans to complete each activity.

Patterning
Glue beans on cardboard to make a pattern. Repeat the pattern several times. Ask a friend to explain your pattern.

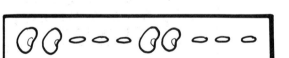

Alphabet/Number Cards
Glue beans in the shape of letters and numbers. Close your eyes and try to name the letter or number by touching it only.

Math Computation

Write math problems on cardboard. Glue beans next to each problem to check your work.

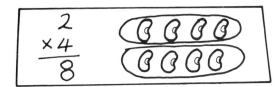

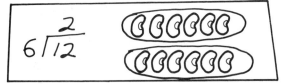

Cursive Writing

Glue beans to cardboard to make large cursive letters. Practice tracing the letters with your fingers each day.

Fractions of a Set

Glue a set of two types of beans to tagboard. Draw a circle around all the beans of one type. Write a fraction to represent the set. The top number of the fraction should be the **part** that is circled. The bottom number should be the **total** number of beans. Make additional cards to show other fractions.

Graphing for Literature

Ask your classmates a question such as "What is your favorite non-fiction book?" or "What was your favorite part of the story?" Design a graph using glued beans to record your classmates' responses.

Other Ideas . . .

- Bean recipes
- Abstract designs
- Holiday pictures
- Historical events

Board Games

Students love to play games. This project will give them a chance to create an enjoyable board game that will help students review curriculum, set up a learning center, or explore new information.

Materials:
- sheet of tagboard or cardboard
- construction paper
- paper clips
- envelopes
- markers, pencils, crayons
- rulers
- plastic bottle caps
- spinner, dice, play money

Directions:
Establish a topic for the game. Have students design boards and cards from art supplies. Students can write rules and cards, and gather game pieces.

Adventures Through the Wild West
Make a game board that depicts the life and times of the pioneers and their travels across the country.

I'd Rather Be At The Mall
Use your knowledge of money to make a game that takes you shopping in the mall.

Discovering the Outdoors

Make a game where you travel through a habitat such as a jungle, rainforest, park, mountain or desert. Use research to make question and answer cards that are factually correct.

Story Setting

Invent a board game that shows the setting of a favorite story or book. Include important events from the beginning, middle, and end. Make cards with questions about the story or instructions telling players to pantomime important events.

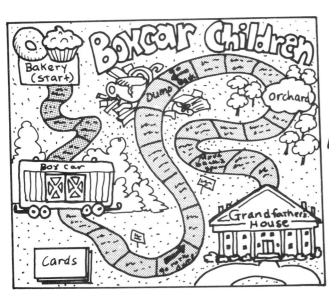

Save the Earth

Design a game that will teach people to care for our earth. Use cards, pictures, and game spaces to share information.

Our Town

Use facts about your community to make a board game that takes players through town.

Other Ideas . . .

- Fairy tales
- Adventures
- Vacation
- Grocery shopping

Cereal Box Reports

Folded paper cereal boxes can become book reports, student introductions, or field trip reports. These make beautiful gift boxes. They can also be used as shelf, center, or hanging displays.

Materials:

- 18" x 24" white construction paper
- scissors
- glue or tape
- colored pencils, crayons, markers, pens
- pattern, p. 86

Directions:

Have students trace the pattern. Instruct them to cut and fold the box to make creases, and decorate the sides and ends. Students can glue or tape the box closed and display the box as appropriate.

Science Cereal

Decorate the box to illustrate a science concept. Use science vocabulary as the ingredients. Write facts on the front and back of the box.

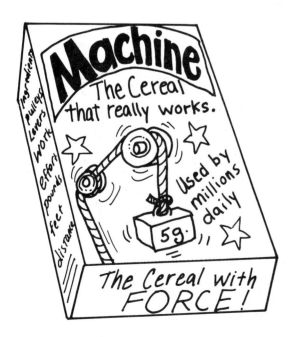

Cereal Introductions

During the first week of school make a box to put yourself "on display." Use the box to tell about your hobbies, likes, dislikes, and special talents.

Field Trip Cereal

Describe a field trip using the box to display a list of what you saw. Write adjectives on the cover. Keep souvenirs and pamphlets inside.

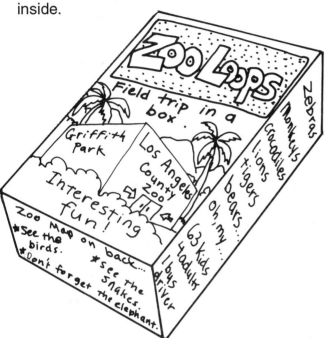

Mystery Cereal

Choose a classmate, book character, athlete, or a famous person as a mystery person. Draw the mystery person's picture on the front of the box. Write descriptions as clues. Hide the mystery person's name inside the box.

Dad or Mom-in-a-Box

Make a unique Father's or Mother's Day card. Design a box to praise all the wonders of Mom and Dad.

Description Cereal

Choose a small object to describe. Decorate the box with adjectives that describe the object. Hide the object in the box. Challenge a friend to guess the object by reading the adjectives.

Other Ideas . . .

- Historical events
- Video and book reports
- Favorite ethnic recipes

Claydough

Claydough provides students with an opportunity to explore their creativity using a unique manipulative. It provides them with a medium to display their talents and mastery of a topic in an exciting and motivating way.

Materials:

- one cup white flour
- one cup water
- two teaspoons cream of tartar
- one cup of salt
- tablespoon of vegetable oil
- food coloring (several drops)
- waxed paper
- air tight container

Directions:

Mix ingredients in a pot. Cook for five minutes over medium heat stirring with a metal spoon. Dough will begin to harden and gather on the spoon. Pour dough on wax paper and let it cool. Knead until smooth. Store dough in airtight containers. It will last about two weeks.

Relief Map

Make a relief map depicting the city, state, or geographic region in which you live.

Math Manipulatives

Design numbers and math symbols from claydough. Practice your math facts using your personally designed manipulatives.

Balanced Meals

Make models of three balanced meals using paper plates and claydough.

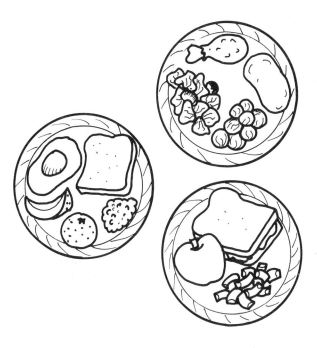

Earth Model

Make a model of the Earth using three colors of claydough to depict the crust mantle, and core. Slice your model in half to reveal the layers. Use toothpicks and small paper flags to label the parts.

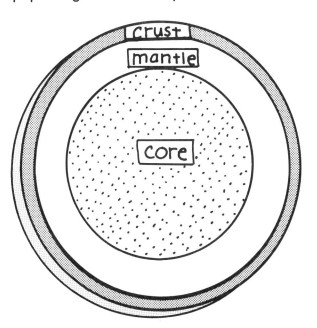

Community Helpers

Make a community helper figure from claydough. Put it on display with a curator card describing that helper's role.

A FIRE FIGHTER....
Is trained in first aid.
Teaches fire prevention classes.
Is on call in case of emergencies.
Risks his life.

Museum of Sculpture

Make a claydough sculpture of a famous figure. Write a curator card to tell about this famous person.

BABE RUTH
1895-1948
.342 batting average
714 homers during his career
one of the first members of the
Baseball Hall of Fame.

Other Ideas . . .

- Food Pyramid
- Math facts
- Historical science
- Famous person

Codes and Symbols

Code and symbol activities can be motivating learning tools. They promote critical thinking and are adaptable for virtually every content area.

Materials:
- patterns, p. 87
- chalkboard, chalk
- writing paper
- pencils
- drawing paper

Directions:
Write a coded message directly on the board or on paper at a work station. Provide a decoding sheet. For some activities students will create their own codes. For coding ideas, see p. 87.

Following Directions
Play "Symbol Says." Decode the message on the board and follow its directions.

Mystery Character
Use a code to describe a literary character. Trade with a friend, decode, and illustrate.

Friendly Letters

Write a coded letter to a classmate. Write your friend's name in code on the top line. Post all the letters on the board. Decode the top line of each letter to find your message.

Rebus Stories

Write a story using rebus symbols. Challenge a friend to decipher your code.

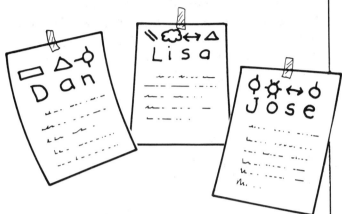

Math

Write and solve math problems that use letters to represent numbers.

A = 1
B = 2
C = 3
D = 4

Science

Write a weather report using coded symbols to represent weather conditions. Research ideas using the weather page of a newspaper.

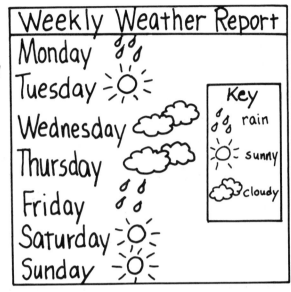

Social Studies

Imagine you're a Native American in the 1800's, just back from your first hunt. Tell your story in pictographs.

Other Ideas . . .

- Parts of speech
- Math stories
- Word Families such as -at; -an; -ip
- Name tags, badges

Currency

Students develop paper money to express their knowledge in various subject areas. At the same time they will learn the concepts of value and exchange.

Materials:
- paper circles for coins
- 8½" x 11" paper
- pencils, crayons, markers
- rulers
- scissors

Directions:
Provide paper circles for coins and instruct students to fold 8½" x 11" paper in thirds, unfold, and cut along the folds to make currency. Have students decorate the bills and coins for each activity.

Literature
Judge the quality of a book you have read by designing currency to show its value. Show your currency to a friend and explain why you chose the denomination and design.

Math
Make currency for a class store. Get permission to bring in items from home or make products to sell.

Science

Demonstrate your understanding of a food chain by using denominations of currency to show each animal's position in the chain. On the back of your currency include facts about the animals.

Historical Currency

Design currency to represent a historical period or explain a specific event from the past.

Self Esteem

Design a series of currency to honor a friend in your class.

Other Ideas . . .

- Rewards and awards
- Prize auction
- Class bank with checks and loans

Dioramas-in-the-Round

Dioramas-in-the-round give students a new way to learn and demonstrate knowledge. Round dioramas are motivating and easy to make. Use them in any curricular area or as decoration.

Materials:
- two or more evenly cut paper or tagboard circles
- pencils, crayons, markers
- scissors
- glue, stapler
- construction paper

Directions:
Have students cut two even circles. Instruct students to fold the circles in half. They place both circles on a desk with two halves resting on the desk, and two halves positioned vertically toward the ceiling. Instruct students to glue the vertical halves of the circles back to back forming the backdrop for a two-sided diorama. The halves on the desk provide bases for 3-D designs. Have students add 3-D designs, glue them to the bases, and decorate the backgrounds.

What's the Difference?
Complete one side of the diorama to make 3-D designs that show what transportation is like today. On the other side show what transportation will be like in the future.

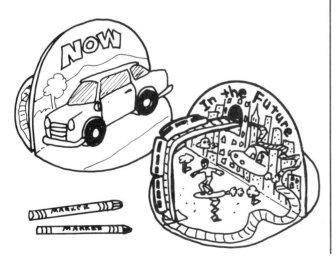

Around The World
Make a two-sided diorama that compares your country to another. 3-D designs can include examples of food, living conditions, celebrations, and traditions.

Hypothesis Versus Results

Complete a science experiment. Make a diorama-in-the-round with one side that demonstrates your hypothesis and another side that shows what actually happened.

Story Comparison

Make a round diorama to show how two stories are alike.

Cause and Effect

Complete the sentence, "If I _____ , then _____ ." Design one side of your diorama to show the "if" part of the sentence, and the other side to illustrate the "then" part.

Math Practice

Choose a math equation such as $3 + 2 = 5$. Write two story problems that demonstrate that equation. Make a diorama-in-the-round with 3-D designs that illustrate each story problem.

Other Ideas . . .

- Book characters
- Sports
- Music styles
- Historical events

Eyeglasses

Glasses can change how we see things. Here are some glasses that help students see what they know.

Materials:
- tagboard or cereal box cardboard
- construction paper
- crayons
- glue
- scissors
- red and green cellophane
- pattern, p. 88

Directions:
Help students use the pattern on p. 88 to trace eyeglasses on tagboard or cardboard. Instruct them to cut out eyeglasses, glue them together, and decorate them for each activity.

Looking At You
Decorate the glasses with your favorite colors. Glue on small cut-outs to represent who you are. Use them to introduce yourself to a friend.

Look to the Future
Design glasses that show your dreams for the future. Attach cut-outs such as the car you will drive, the career you will have, or the house you will buy.

Stages of Blindness

Insert wax paper lenses into your glasses. Walk about the room carefully or choose a trusted friend to lead you. Write a description of your experience. Cover the lenses with black paper and repeat the activity. Write a story to explain what you discovered.

Career Day

Study careers in which protective glasses are important to complete a task. Pick a career such as a pilot, welder, machinist, or dentist. Design glasses and give a presentation about your career.

Magic Glasses

Make magic 3-D glasses. Cut two holes in the center of the glasses. Cover one hole with red cellophane and one with green cellophane. Then decorate. Describe your vision using only adjectives.

Animal Glasses

Decorate glasses to be an animal mask. Research the animal and give an oral presentation while wearing the glasses.

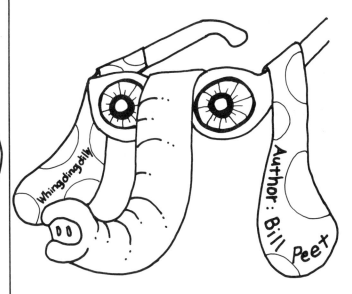

Book Report Bifocals

Decorate glasses to represent a favorite character in a story. Wear your glasses and retell the story from the character's point of view.

Other Ideas . . .

- Hundred's Day glasses (decorated with 100 things)
- Invention glasses (with added features such as wipers, antennas, or defoggers)
- Gift glasses

Face-Fact Plates

Students can design a paper plate face about new concepts or facts. It's fun to exchange the plates or display them on an interactive bulletin board.

Materials:
- paper plates, one per student
- construction paper
- scissors
- glue
- small plastic bags for pockets

Directions:
Have students use a paper plate for the face. Instruct them to design facial features from construction paper. They can write clues or a question on the nose, and the answer on the tongue. Then students should roll the tongue pattern around a pencil to create a spiral. Students can attach the features with tape or glue. If one face requires multiple noses and tongues, have students make a storage pocket by taping

Math Facts
Make multiple noses and tongues. Write math facts on the noses. Write the answers on the tongues.

Book Characters
Describe a favorite book character on the nose. Name the character on the tongue.

Geography

Write the definition of a landform or a geographical location on the nose. Hide the name under the tongue.

Contractions

Write contractions on interchangeable noses. Make multiple tongues with the long form of each contraction.

Sentence Structure

Write a sentence on the nose. Underline one word in the sentence. List its part of speech, such as noun, verb, or adjective, on the tongue.

Historical Facts

On the nose, write a question about an historical event such as an important discovery, invention, birth, or death. Write the answer on the tongue.

Science

Create a "mad scientist" face. Write science questions and answers on the nose and tongue.

Other Ideas . . .

- Shape names
- Community helpers
- States and capitals
- Synonyms and antonyms

Fact Catchers

Fact catchers can be used for a variety of activities. They can serve as a tool for curriculum review, a research activity, a fact finder, or an ice breaker. Students can use fact catchers independently or with partners.

Materials:
- scissors
- 8½" x 8½" square sheet of paper
- pencil, pen
- markers, crayons
- directions, p. 89

Directions:
1. Have students make the fact catchers by the following directions on p. 89.
2. Instruct students to write the numbers one, two, three, and four on the finger pockets.
3. Have students write four questions, statements, or words on the triangular top flaps of the fact catchers for each activity.
4. Instruct students to write responses to what has been written on the back side of each corresponding top flap.

To Play:
The holder puts a thumb or forefinger from each hand into each finger pocket so that the fact catcher is closed. The player selects a number from the finger pockets. The holder pinches the fact catcher in and out counting until the number is reached. The player selects one question, statement, or word that he or she has seen on a flap and responds to it. The holder looks under the flap to check for the correct response.

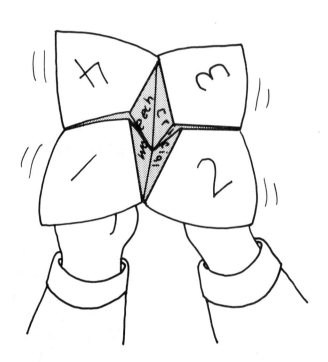

Word Catcher
Write four vocabulary words on the top flaps and the correct definition under each word. Quiz a partner.

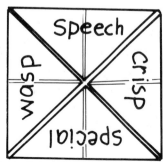

Getting to Know You

Write four categories such as favorite movies, books, food, or places on the top flaps. Under the flaps write your favorite example in each category. Have a classmate try to guess what you've written.

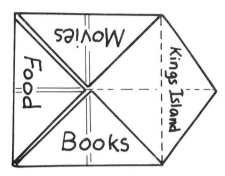

Class Catcher

Make a fact catcher with top flaps that highlight four class events such as field trips, assemblies, concerts or visitors. Write a sentence about why you liked each event under the top flaps. Share the fact catcher with visitors during Open House.

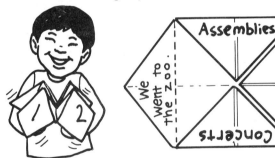

Transportation Past and Present

Write four questions on the top flaps, one for each mode of transportation: sea, land, air, and space. Write the answers under each flap. Use the fact catcher to teach a friend about transportation.

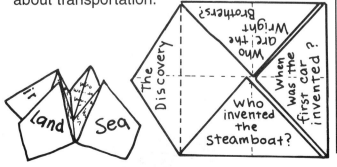

Science

Choose one science topic such as rocks and minerals, plants, or electricity. On the top flaps of the fact catcher, write four true or false statements regarding the topic. Under each flap write the correct answer. Challenge a classmate to guess if the statements are true or false.

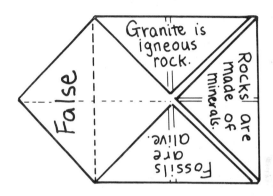

Math Families

Write four math problems—one for each math operation: addition, subtraction, multiplication, and division on the top flaps of the fact catcher. Write the answers under the top flaps. Use the fact catcher to help a friend practice math facts.

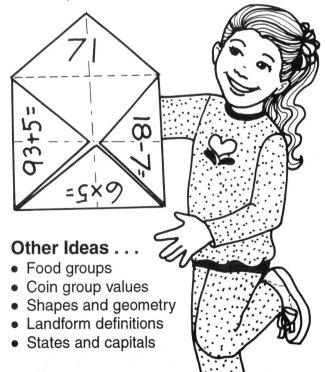

Other Ideas . . .

- Food groups
- Coin group values
- Shapes and geometry
- Landform definitions
- States and capitals

Fence Weaving

Many schools have chain-link fences. Designs and messages woven into the fence fabric create large sculptures that everyone will enjoy.

Materials:
- chain-link fencing
- butcher paper, crepe paper, cellophane
- graph paper for planning designs

Directions:
Assign cooperative groups. Have students in each group turn their graph paper on a diagonal, draw designs, and choose a design to weave into the fence. Instruct them to weave crepe paper, cellophane, or rolled butcher paper in and out of a chain-link fence to produce their designs.

Geometric Figures
Weave geometric designs into the fence. Use the holes to measure and compare the area and perimeter of the designs.

Welcome Sign
Weave a message into the fence to welcome a special visitor to your school.

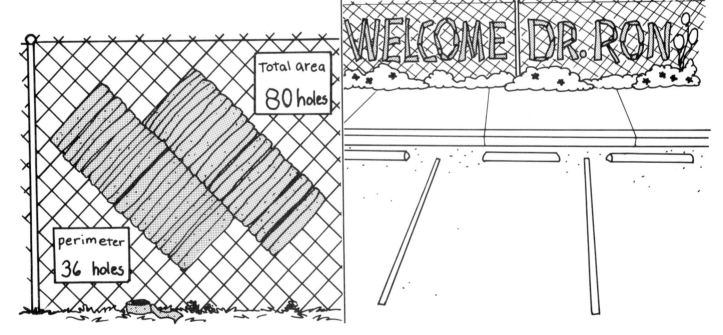

Total area
80 holes

perimeter
36 holes

Holidays Fence

Weave symbols of holidays such as pumpkins, pine trees, hearts, or Abraham Lincoln. Hang a sign that names each symbol and the holiday it represents.

Math

Given the average length and height of an animal, research how to make a weaving of the animal that is to scale. Make the fence weaving and design a sign to hang from the fence that tells the animal's actual length and height.

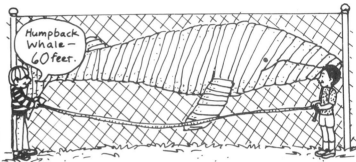

Language Arts

Fence weave backdrops for outdoor play performances.

Social Studies

Fence weave a flow chart with symbols representing three historical events in order. Design hanging signs that define each weaving.

Other Ideas . . .
- Boundary or goal for a P.E. game
- Ad for fund raiser
- Story sequence

File Folder Books

File folders are sturdy and make great book covers and pages. They can be used for reports, summaries, and/or portfolios. When laminated, file folder books become quite durable.

Materials:
- blank file folders
- stapler
- pencil, crayons, markers
- writing paper
- construction paper
- glue
- blank paper

Directions:
Select the number of folders desired for the activity. Have students label the folder with their names and decorate for the activity. Have the students label the tabs so that books can be filed alphabetically into a central resource file.

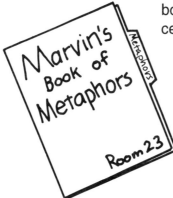

Book Map
Design a cover for your favorite story on the front. Make a book map by illustrating the story plot on the inside. On the back, tell why you recommend the book.

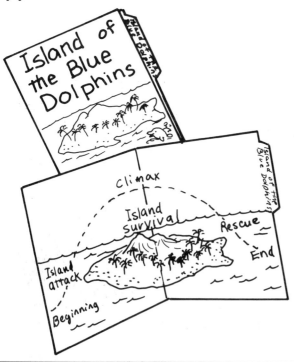

Picture Books
Work in a cooperative group to make a picture book. Use several file folders to make the pages. Write large and fill the pages with illustrations. Staple the pages together. Share your book with other groups.

Career Portfolio

Interview two or three people who have the same kind of job. Write a career portfolio and enter it in a job fair.

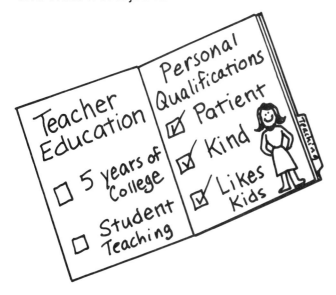

Shape Book

Cut your file folder in a shape that is related to a story. Trim all your pages to fit the same shape and then write your story.

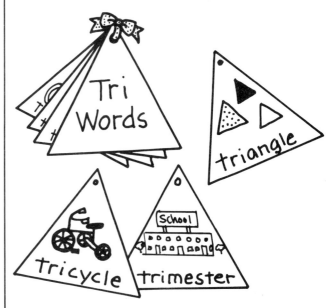

Animal Kingdoms

Create a reference file for your favorite animal kingdom. Use an encyclopedia to research each kingdom.

Biographies

Choose a favorite sports star, author, or musician. Write a biography for your star. Illustrate the cover with an event from your star's life.

Other Ideas . . .

- Curricular reports
- Portfolios
- Poster books
- Art display book
- Bookmaking center

Flip-Flop Books

Creatively folded flip-flop books progress from cover to ending in a clock-wise unfolding manner. Flip-flop books are an excellent tool for language arts and can be used in science and social studies as well. The final opening presents an 18" x 18" drawing.

Materials:

- glue
- three 18" x 18" sheets of construction paper
- tape
- scissors
- colored pencils
- 8½" x 8½" white lined paper inserts
- directions, p. 90

Directions:

Folding and cutting directions can be found on p. 90. Attach neatly completed, numbered inserts on correct pages.

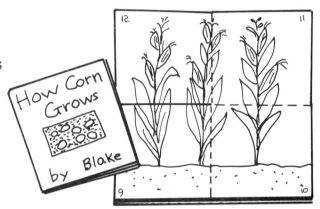

Progressive Story

Tell a story which takes the main character through many settings. The story should unfold from the cover through page 15. Use the final opened sheet to reveal the climax as a giant 18" x 18" picture.

Mystery Me

Write fifteen clues about yourself and reveal who you are on the last page.

Time Line

Design a time line about a period or event in history. For example, you might use fifteen pages to reveal the progress of flight—with the finale a picture of a space station.

Museum of Art

Feature an artist of your choice on the cover. Tell about his or her life on the pages. Simulate his or her work as the "center fold."

Important Events

Describe important events in a historical time period or in your family's life.

Group Flip-Flops

Work together with a cooperative group to plan and make a flip-flop book about your group's unique characteristics.

Other Ideas . . .

- Fewer pages
- Circle books made by trimming corners
- Additional sheets for a class book
- Field trip reports

Hands

"Handy" shapes can be used as tools to organize, display, communicate, and review information.

Materials:
- paper
- pencils, crayons
- stapler
- colored construction paper, 9" x 12"
- glue
- writing paper, cut 6" x 8"
- drawing paper

Directions:
Have students place their hands on colored construction paper. Direct them to carefully trace around their hand and fingers to make a pattern. Have them cut out patterns to use with the activities below.

Shake Hands with Your Favorite Character

Shake hands with your favorite book character. Sketch the character's picture or write his or her most important qualities on one hand and then yours on the other. Attach the hands as shown.

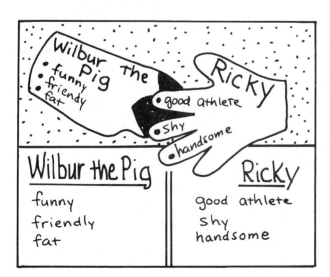

Helping Hands Award

Decorate your hand to reward someone who has helped you.

Math Facts at the Tips of Your Fingers

Cut out two matching hands. Glue them together leaving the fingers free. Practice your math facts by writing a math fact on each finger.

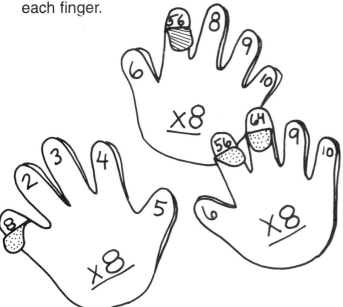

Friendship Circle

Record your talents and interests on the fingers of a cut-out hand. Work with a cooperative group to glue your hands into a friendship circle.

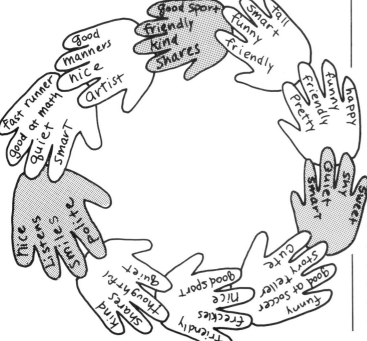

Jobs for Hands

Write a paragraph about a specific job hands can do. Trace, cut out, and glue pairs of hands on drawing paper. Illustrate the hands to show them performing the task.

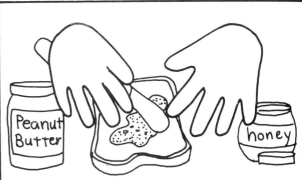

My hands can make a sandwich. First spread peanut butter. Next comes honey. Then my hands pick it up to eat.

Artsy hands

Trace and cut out one hand. Glue the hand on a piece of drawing paper. Imagine the hand as a part of a picture related to literature. Draw in the remaining parts.

Johnny Appleseed

Other Ideas . . .

- Hand It To Ya' Awards
- Book covers
- Counting by 5s and 10s
- Holidays
- Flowers

Hangers

Hangers may be used for book reports, research reports, and field trip summaries. Hangers can be covered with a variety of materials and made into mobiles, used for decoration, as centers, or for recording and sharing new information.

Materials:

- wire hangers
- construction paper, fabric, or contact paper
- scissors
- string
- pencils, pens
- markers
- glue
- stapler
- hole puncher

Directions:

Students should bend the hanger into the desired shape and cover the opening of the hanger with the material of their choice.

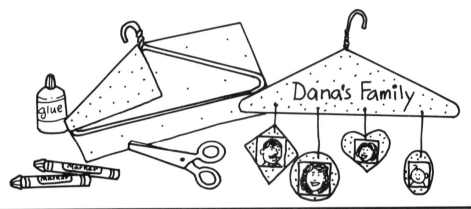

Book Reports

Draw an illustration for a book you've read. Write a summary of the book on the back highlighting story elements, such as setting, characters, plot and sequence.

Science Topics

Select a topic such as tide pools. On one side draw a picture of four tidepool animals. On the other side write the names and descriptions of each animal. Hang additional examples of tidepool life as desired.

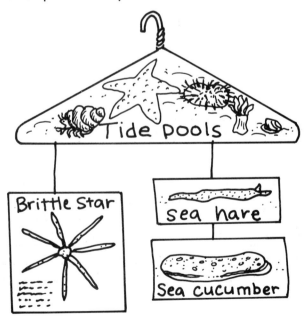

Art

Select a medium of art to display on a hanger frame. Bend the hanger to be the frame and display your artwork.

Geometric Shapes

Reshape coat hangers into triangles, circles, squares and free form shapes before covering. Place the name of the shape on one side. Glue photographed examples of the shape cut out from magazines on the other side.

State Geography

Select geographic regions such as deserts, mountains, valleys, or bodies of water. On one side of the hanger draw a map of the state selected. On the opposite side write a brief statement about each region found in that state.

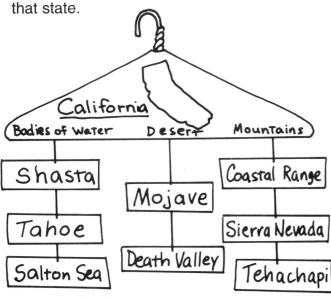

Other Ideas . . .

- Advertisements
- Student government posters
- Who's who (wanted posters)
- Research report
- Wire sculpture
- Holidays

Headbands

Headbands can be used to record information, practice facts, or express opinions.

Materials:

- adding machine tape
- pencils, crayons
- glue, tape, or staples

Directions:

Cut strips of tape about 18 inches long. Make strips available to students for each activity. Headbands can be joined with glue, tape, or staples.

Math Bands

Write a family of math facts around your headband. Attach a shape in the middle to identify the math family.

Science

Record an interesting science fact related to the unit you are studying. Find two class-mates who wrote a fact related to yours.

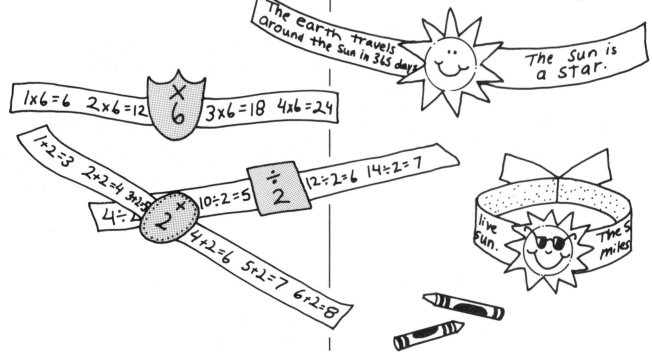

100 Day Headbands

Make a 100 day headband where the zeros become glasses. Write your 100s from zero to 1,000.

Mystery Characters

Put the name of a character on a headband. Put the headband on a friend's head without showing him or her the character's name. Challenge your friend to ask "yes" or "no" questions to get clues about the character until he or she can guess the character's identity.

Circumference Headband

Make your headband into a ruler. Predict and measure your partner's head.

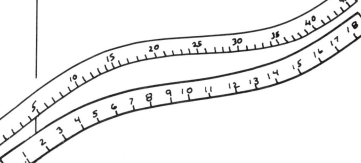

Mystery Books

Write or draw something on your headband to represent your favorite story. Read your classmates' headbands. Try to guess their favorite stories.

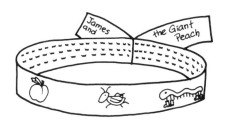

Alphabet Bands

Write the alphabet on your headband. Draw a picture that starts with each letter.

Other Ideas . . .

- Headbands for holidays
- Healthy habits
- Food groups
- Teams for P.E.

"I Am..." Cards

Simple cards can help students identify with what they are learning. Students might use "I am" cards to hold an "I am" parade, to make oral presentations or to play guessing games.

Materials:

- 9" x 6" construction paper
- hole puncher
- ribbon or yarn
- markers, crayons
- pencil, pen

Directions:

Students write "I Am . . ." at the top of their card. For each activity children can decorate and write facts about who they are on their cards.

Math Facts

Choose a math sign such as =, +, or x . Write the sign in the middle of the card. Add words, pictures or equations to show the meaning of the sign.

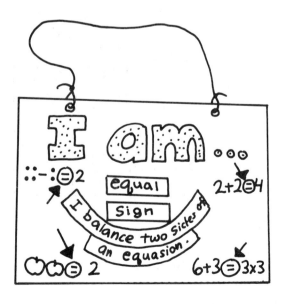

Parts of Speech

Choose a part of speech such as verb, noun, or adjective. Fill your card with words that are from that part of speech.

MORE Alternative to Worksheets Creative Teaching Press

All About Me!

Write your name in the middle of the card. Make designs around your name that will tell who you are, what you like, and your special talents.

Historical Figure

Draw a picture of an historical figure in the center of your card. Write his or her name under the picture and illustrate important life events.

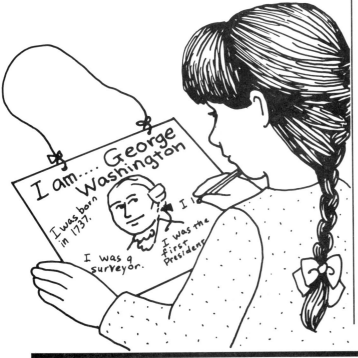

Mythological Characters

Design a card about a mythological character. Include information about his or her role in mythology, such as Poseidon, Greek god of the waters, brother of Zeus.

Book Character

Draw a portrait of a book character. Use designs and sentences to tell what the character does in the story.

Other Ideas . . .

- Character traits
- Community helpers
- Political figures
- Endangered Species

Light Switch Covers

Light switch covers give students a chance to write reminders to themselves or others. Switch covers are easily seen, interactive, and can be used every day at home or school.

Materials:
- construction paper
- markers, crayons, colored chalk
- scissors
- clear tape
- pattern, p. 91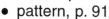

Directions:
Reproduce pattern on p. 91. Have students design and illustrate their cover. Students then cut out the light switch cover and tape it in place.

Conservation
Design a switch cover illustrating a conservation theme.

Day Brighteners
Decorate a switch cover to encourage a friend, family member, or school worker.

Words of Wisdom

Research a famous saying from *Aesop's Fables, Poor Richard's Almanac*, or a world leader. Record the quote on a switch cover and tell a friend what your quote means.

Homework Habits

Make switch cover advertisements to remind students to bring in their homework.

Healthy Reminders

Make school kitchen and lunchroom covers that encourage good eating habits.

Book Advertisement

Advertise your favorite book with a light switch cover. Work with a cooperative group to make a billboard called, *Turn on the Lights and Read* to display your ads.

Other Ideas . . .

- Factual information
- Special events
- Reward for good behavior

Magazine Cut-ups

Using pictures from magazines gives students a creative way to demonstrate their knowledge through activities that go beyond cut-and-paste.

Materials:
- magazines, catalogues
- construction paper
- glue
- stapler
- pencils, crayons, markers
- scissors
- white paper
- coin stamps (optional)

Directions:
Ask students to collect magazines and catalogues. Students work individually or in groups to cut out and use pictures they choose in each activity.

Math Shopping
Cut out pictures of things you want to buy. Glue the pictures to construction paper. Draw a price tag for each item. Write and solve an addition problem to show the total cost for all the items.

Selling an Item
Use a picture cut from a magazine to make an advertisement for a product. Include important product information and persuasive writing in your ad.

Old and New

Draw a line to divide a poster in half. Cut three pictures of clothing or furniture from magazines and glue them to one half. On the second half of your poster, draw similar items from the past. Label every item with its name and dates when it was used.

Estimation

Cut out items from a catalogue and record their prices. Find items that when added together will equal even dollar amounts. Use a calculator to check your work.

Historical Catalogues

Make a catalogue representing a specific time period or historical event.

Coin Stamps

Cut out items pictured in a magazine. Glue the pictures on paper. Use coin stamps or coin drawings to show the value of the items on your paper.

Other Ideas . . .

- Healthy foods
- Vehicles
- Human-made vs. nature-made
- Things made of cloth
- Gifts for family members

Menus

Working with menus is a real-life opportunity for children to learn about business and health. Help students explore, analyze, and design menus that can be used for more than just ordering food.

Materials:
- menus from restaurants
- writing paper
- drawing paper
- pencils, crayons, markers
- paper plates, paper cups, plastic utensils
- calorie counter books

Directions:
Collect a variety of authentic menus and have students design their own to complete a selected activity.

Please and Thank You
Work with a cooperative group to set up a classroom restaurant. Give a demonstration on polite ordering and friendly service. Take turns being waiter and customer, serving the food, and calculating the bill.

How Many Calories Did I Have?
Copy a favorite meal from a menu. Use a calorie counter to compute the amount of calories in the meal. Research and compare your results to the number of calories recommended for a student your age.

Calories by Ted	
Fried Shrimp	298
Rice	130
Lettuce	30
Dressing	158
Milk	80
total calories	696

Healthy Eating

Research the contents for a nutritious breakfast. Use a breakfast menu and order a healthy meal.

Historical Menus

Design a menu for a time in history or for a dinner at the White House. Include food from all the food groups.

Family Night Out

Use a menu to plan a family dinner at a restaurant. Write an order for each member of your family. Compute the total cost with tax.

Menu Thinking Game

Find three ways to sort a stack of menus into categories. Explain your sorting rules to a friend. Challenge your friend to find one more sorting rule.

Other Ideas . . .
- Healthy diet
- Menu for different states, countries
- Menu art
- Class book of restaurant names and logos

Murals

Murals set the scene for learning. Students must gather information and cooperate to complete a mural that conveys a message or an idea clearly and cleverly.

Materials:

- butcher paper
- markers, paint, crayons

Directions:

Group students in teams of three or four. Provide a large sheet of butcher paper for each team. Have teams assign roles and work together to plan and make a mural on a central theme. Encourage students to use all of the space available to show information in detail.

Giving Directions

Choose something you do every day such as brushing your teeth or eating cereal. Make a mural that depicts each step to complete the task, and give an oral report using the mural as a visual aid.

Add On Mural

You are the "Student Artist of the Day." Illustrate today's chapter from the read-aloud or today's lesson in science or math. Each day have friends take turns adding to the mural to make a pictorial summary of the whole book or unit of study.

"I'm a Part of History" Mural

Design a mural which follows a historical event through time. Label each important person, place, or thing. Put yourself into the mural event and write captions to tell what you saw.

Story Problems

Choose a math equation such as $10 - 4 = 6$. Divide the mural in half and in each section tell a story to demonstrate that equation.

Science

Create a mural that details a volcano erupting or a spacecraft launching. Include more than one view and important facts to explain your illustrations.

Fact Mural

Choose a topic you are just beginning to study such as the desert, space exploration, or the American Revolution. Design a mural to illustrate the topic. Write one or two facts on the mural that you already know about the topic. Hang the mural. Each day, add new facts to the mural. Use the mural as a review before a test.

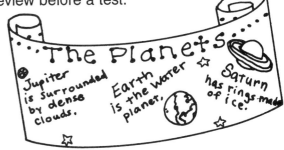

Other Ideas . . .

- Class friendship mural
- Healthy habits mural
- Classroom events mural
- Writing process mural
- Insect mural

Necklaces

Children can wear their knowledge! Students make a necklace with charms that highlight what they are learning.

Materials:

- 30" to 36" string per child
- construction paper
- crayons, markers
- beads, macaroni or other "creative jewels"
- hole punch for charms
- scissors

Directions:

Decide on the topic for the necklace. Have students design a set of charms that reinforce the topic. They can alternate charms, beads, macaroni and other creative jewels as they string the necklace for each activity.

Me, Myself, and I

Design a necklace that shows all the facets of your personality. Try to include every color of the rainbow.

My Community

Make a necklace of the most important buildings in your community. Design and string the buildings between beads. Then take a friend on a tour of your necklace.

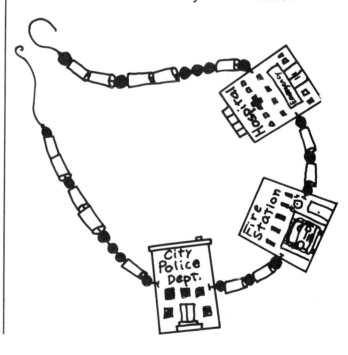

Number Necklaces

Write several math problems that all have the same answer. Use the problems to decorate your necklace. Challenge a friend to find your secret number.

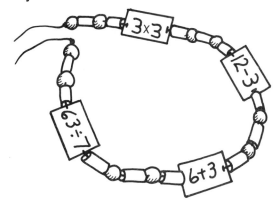

Pattern Necklaces

Design a necklace using patterns of shapes, colors, or numbers. Write a story about how the pattern necklace helped a child in trouble.

Science Scramble

Make a necklace that scrambles an important vocabulary word. Have a partner unscramble your necklace, restring it and tell you the definition.

Sequencing

Illustrate the main events in a story and string them in correct order on the necklace.

Hero Award

Choose a local hero that you would like to honor with a necklace award. Spotlight his or her achievements on a necklace and formally present the necklace to your hero.

Other Ideas . . .

- Holiday fun
- States
- Adjectives

Paper Dolls

Paper dolls help children express themselves. Dolls can be used in storytelling, demonstrations, and conflict management. They encourage students to interact and to experiment with new ideas.

Materials:
- colored construction paper
- scraps of material
- scissors
- glue
- drawing paper
- writing paper
- pencils, crayons, markers
- pattern, p. 92

Directions:
Have students use the pattern on p. 92 or make dolls of their own design. Children should cut out the doll and decorate it to fit the activity.

My Body
Choose a body system such as the skeletal system, digestive system, or nervous system. Draw the system on your doll. Label the parts.

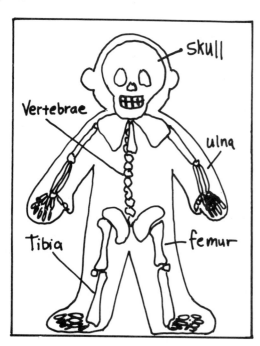

Community Helpers
Make your doll into a community helper. Write a paragraph about that career.

Best Friends

Make a chain of paper dolls. Fold a long piece of paper into fourths like a fan. Trace the doll pattern on the paper so both hands and feet are against the folds. Cut out the doll chain, but do not cut where the hands and feet are joined. Open the chain, decorate the dolls, and write a story about four friends.

Athletes

Choose a real or imaginary sport. Design a sports doll and make sports equipment. Write the rules of the game.

People in History

Design and dress your doll to be a Civil War soldier. Research the Civil War to show the real uniform.

Family Gifts

Use the pattern to make dolls of your family. Decorate the dolls to honor family members. Glue each doll to the front of a sheet of paper folded like a greeting card. Write a message to a family member inside the card.

Other Ideas . . .

- Seasonal clothing
- Holiday clothing
- Presidents
- School personnel
- My hero
- Mother's or Father's Day card

Passports

Student-made passports offer an exciting way to record information. Students use knowledge and imagination to design passports that describe a tourist's travels through a new location.

Materials:
- construction paper, 6" x 9"
- paper, 8½" x 5½"
- stamps and stamp pads (optional)

Directions:
Have students fold 6" x 9" construction paper in half to make a passport cover and staple 8½" x 5½" paper inside for pages. Students design passports for each activity.

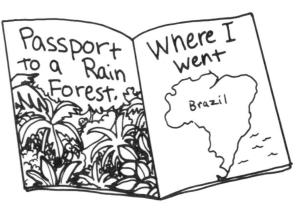

Book Character
Make a passport to explain a favorite book character's role in a story. Make pages to explain the character's travels through settings and events in the book.

Science
Imagine you are a tourist traveling through a specific habitat. Make a passport that shows where you went, when you were there, what the weather conditions were, and what you saw.

Into the Future

Design a passport for a person visiting your country in the year 2100. Have the passport show any changes in spoken language, land borders, and modes of travel. Include an imaginary journal about the character's trip.

Cultures

Imagine you are traveling through a foreign country. Design a passport to show where you have been, what you have seen, and what you have experienced.

Social Studies

Make a passport for a famous historical figure. Have the pages show where the person has been and what was accomplished during their travels.

Library Tour

Make a passport to explain a tour through the library. On each page, describe a part of the library, such as the fiction section, reference area, card catalogue or media center. Include reasons for traveling to that section and examples of literature and materials found there.

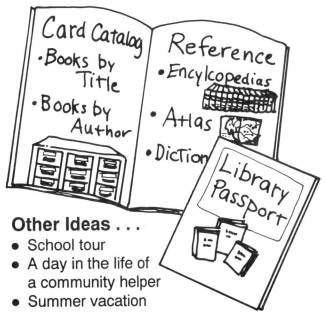

Other Ideas . . .

- School tour
- A day in the life of a community helper
- Summer vacation

Pencil Holders

Students design simple 3-sided pencil holders for their desks. The holders are a great way to record key facts, ideas, or reminders.

Materials:
- scissors
- clear tape
- markers, crayons
- index cards
- pattern, p. 93

Directions:
Have students design the pattern, cut it out and assemble it according to the pattern directions. Students tape "flaps" to index cards to make bottoms for the holders. Have students tape index cards and holders to the desks. The holders are used to store supplies.

Smart Start
Use the side panels to record three goals for the school year.

The Writing Process
Record the steps in the writing process.

Word Bank

Keep a list of words you have trouble spelling on the sides of your pencil holder. Practice spelling the words each day.

This is ME!

Describe yourself in three ways.

The Scientific Method

Write out the steps of the scientific method. After each step give a definition.

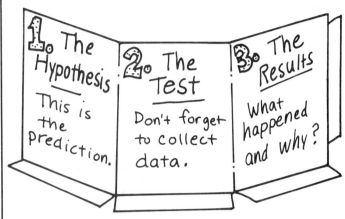

Past, Present, and Future Verbs

Choose five verbs. Write them in the past tense on one side of the holder. Write the same verbs in the present and future tense on the two remaining sides.

Other Ideas . . .

- Sequencing
- Life cycles
- Forms of transportation
- New Year's resolutions

Pinwheels

Pinwheels are fun and motivational for children. They can be used for recording and reviewing factual information as well as for partner quizzes.

Materials:

- scissors
- one new pencil per child
- one thumbtack per child
- markers, crayons
- pattern, p. 94

Directions:

Have students cut out the pinwheel pattern. Students can write answers on the inside triangles and answers on the outside flaps. Then they assemble the pinwheel and share!

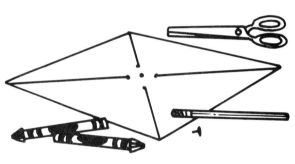

Science

Write examples of groups of animals, such as amphibians, mammals, or reptiles on the outside flaps. Challenge a friend to name the animal group you chose.

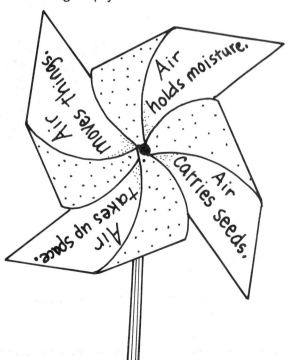

Homonym Hum . . .

Use the inside triangle spaces to write definitions of homonyms and the overlying "flap" to write the words.

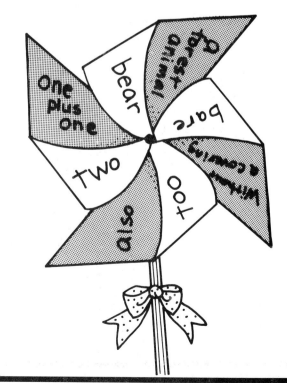

Social Studies

Write the names of four famous explorers on the outside flaps and what each explorer discovered on the inside triangle.

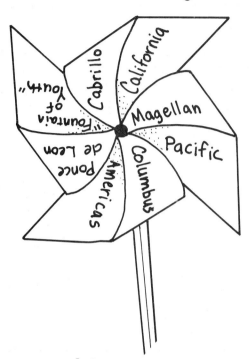

Math

Write math problems on the inside flaps and answers on the outside triangles.

Language Arts

Design a pinwheel to show your knowledge of a book character.

Other Ideas . . .

- Pinwheels gifts
- Pinwheels introductions
- Gift decorations

Placemats

Placemats are a fun way to bring learning to the lunch table or from school to home. Students create a personal placemat that reinforces the topic being studied.

Materials:
- 9" x 12" construction paper
- markers, paint or crayons
- clear contact paper (or laminator)

Directions:
Have students design a placemat that illustrates and summarizes the theme being studied. Cover completed placemats with clear contact paper or laminate them.

Your State
Draw or trace a map of your state. Identify the capital and the town you live in. Add the state bird, flower, or seal or make the entire placement your state flag!

Literature
Illustrate your favorite scene from a book of your choice. Design a simple border to frame your placemat made with the faces of the main characters in your book.

My Family

Design a placemat for each member of your family. Draw their portrait in the center. List positive character traits, hobbies and talents in the border of your placemat.

Holiday Placemats

Make sets of holiday placemats to use at class parties throughout the year. Be sure to make extras for special guests that may visit or for new students who enroll later in the year.

Good Manners

Create a placemat that reminds people to use good table manners.

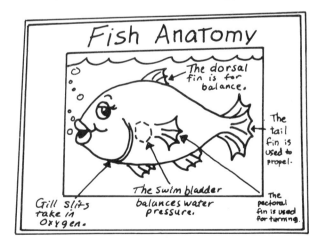

Science

In the center of the placemat, illustrate a science concept you are studying. List key facts that go along with this concept to border your illustration.

Other Ideas . . .

- Food Pyramid
- Math facts
- Historical science
- Famous person

Puppets

Puppets can be used for drama, oral communication, sharing, and/or teaching new concepts and ideas. Puppets encourage oral participation and minimize inhibitions. They allow students to role play characters and to step into other historical eras.

Materials:

- empty plastic dishwashing liquid bottle
- paper
- fabric scraps
- crayons, markers
- buttons, beads, beans
- yarn, string, cotton
- scissors, glue
- stick
- newspaper

Directions:

Students cover the bottle with paper or fabric. They design the face and clothing to fit a real or imaginary character.

Theatre Performance

Perform a puppet play about a character who learns an important lesson about friendship, sharing, or safety.

Problem-Solving Puppeteers

Make up math problems that use the concepts you have been studying. Use the puppets to quiz your classmates.

Mad Scientist

Make a puppet that resembles a mad scientist. Use this puppet to explain an important science concept.

Self-Expression

Make a puppet of yourself. Use the puppet to introduce yourself to the class or to tell about something important.

Book Talk

Make a character from a book you have read. Tell the class about the book using the bottle puppet.

Conflict Resolution

Perform a puppet play that shows how to resolve a problem you might have on the playground, in class, or at home.

Other Ideas . . .

- Holiday plays
- Fairytale theatre
- Music concerts
- Community helpers

Report Cards

What better fun than to have the children make and fill out report cards for assessment. This can provide insight into the way your children think, how they view things, and what qualities they value.

Materials:

- ditto paper or white lined paper
- pencils, pens
- reproductions of actual report cards

Directions:

Encourage students to think carefully about who or what they are grading. Encourage them to write fair and honest assessments from their point of view.

Character Cards

Send a book character a report card to let him or her know what you think of his or her behavior.

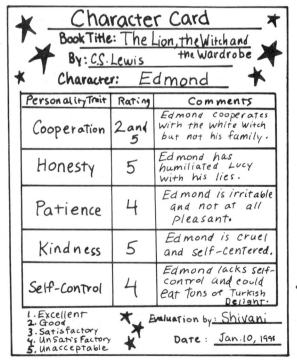

Self-Assessment

Fill out a copy of your report card to let your teacher know how you think you're doing and why.

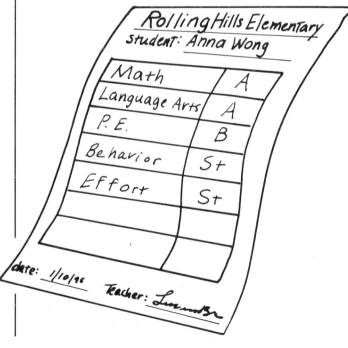

President Grade

Send Mrs. Lincoln a report card on her son Abraham.

Report Card

for: Abraham Lincoln

Childhood: Well behaved
honest
a good reader

Adulthood: humble
good orator
fair and just

Presidency: Stood strong
through the most
difficult of times.

Video Grade

Make a report card to show what you learned from a video shown in class.

Name of Movie: _____
Student: _____
Interest Level
High   Medium   Low
Why? _____
I now know!
1. _____
2. _____
3. _____
Too long , Too short ,
Just right
Best Part: _____

Home Recycling Report

Make a card to be used at home or at school to increase recycling awareness.

Are We Recycling At Home?

	Yes	No	Some
Glass	☒		
Aluminum		☒	
Newspaper	☒		
Water			☒
Cardboard			☒
Wood			☒

My Playground Report

Use a report card to evaluate your own playground behavior.

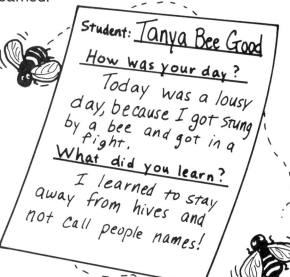

Playground Report

Name: Sarah

Arguments?   some ☒
             none ☐
             a lot ☐

Restroom   first ☐
and drink?   wait ☒
             during recess ☐

Line behavior?
             straight ☒
             quiet ☒
             wild ☐

Comments
there was
he recess,
wait till
before I
the bath.
will try
careful.
Sarah

Report on the Day

Report how your day went and what you learned.

Student: Tanya Bee Good

How was your day?
Today was a lousy day, because I got stung by a bee and got in a fight.

What did you learn?
I learned to stay away from hives and not call people names!

Other Ideas . . .

- Mayor's report card
- Father's or Mother's Day report card
- Friendship report card

Sandwich Boards

Students make wearable, two-sided posters that convey messages, sell products, or relay information to others.

Materials:

- sheets of poster board 28" x 22" for large sandwich boards
- two sheets of construction paper for small sandwich boards
- two lengths of strong rope or yarn
- markers, crayons
- hole puncher

Directions:

Instruct students to create a sandwich board that conveys the message of the unit or theme you are studying. Remind students to print in clear, bold letters. Punch two holes in the top of each board. Connect the ends of each string to the front board and back board.

Health and Safety Board

Advertise a good habit on the front board and tell about that habit on the back.

Book Covers

Design a front and back cover for your favorite book. Summarize the plot on the back. Become a "walking ad" for this book at a literature event.

Before and After

Make a board to show the changes that occurred with an historical event. Show "before" on the front and "after" on the back. Wear at a historical parade.

School Events

Construct a sandwich board that announces an upcoming school event. Use persuasive writing and slogans to encourage students to attend.

Step Into History

Step into history and convince classmates to become a Pony Express rider, an abolitionist, or a gold miner!

Sentence Scrambles

Scramble a sentence for your classmates. See how long it takes them to unscramble it!

Other Ideas . . .
- Endangered Species
- Famous Persons
- Ecology Sandwich Board

Sentence Strip Books

Sentence strip books may be used in a variety of ways for all readers, especially beginning and emergent readers. They are handy tools for teaching word families, sentence structure, and sight vocabulary. Sentence strip books also boost confidence in reading fluency.

Materials:

- blank word cards, index cards, or cut up sentence strips
- whole sentence strips
- scissors
- pencils, crayons, markers
- stapler

Directions:

Students make books by stapling several completed word cards to a sentence strip. Books can be kept in a central location for students to share.

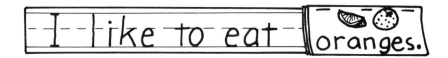

Color Words

Draw several objects of a specific color on blank cards. Write the name below each object. Staple the pile cards to the sentence strip. Practice reading your color book with a friend.

Initial Sounds

Choose one letter of the alphabet. Use cards to draw and label pictures of things that start with that letter. On the sentence strip, write the beginning of a sentence such as, "L is for ____." Finish the sentence by stapling the pile of word cards to the end of the sentence strip.

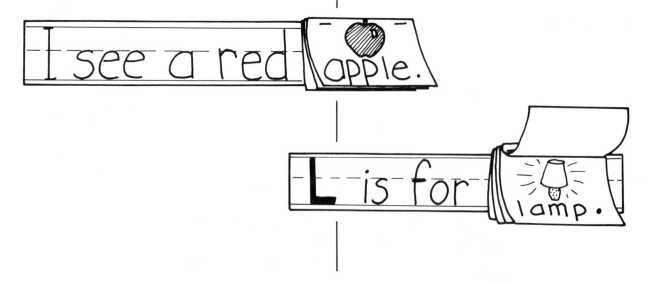

Science Books

Select a science theme to draw and write about. Use five sentence strips stapled together. Illustrate one idea on each strip.

Silly Sentences

Write and illustrate several subjects and several predicates on sentence strips. Mix and match to make funny sentences.

The big dog | jumped rope.
The fiesty gorilla | danced a jig.
My friend Mary | chewed a bone.
The leprechaun | ate a banana.

Holiday Books

Choose a holiday. On a sentence strip, write the beginning of a sentence such as, "On Halloween we see _____." Write or draw a set of cards to finish this sentence. Staple the pile of cards at the end of the sentence strip.

Math Storybooks

Write part of an equation such as 10 − ___ = ___ on a sentence strip. Make two sets of several cards, one set for the middle number, and one for the answer. Arrange the sets in two piles to correctly complete the equation. Staple the sets in the proper places on the sentence strip. Use a blank sheet to cover the answer section. Quiz yourself. Then quiz a friend.

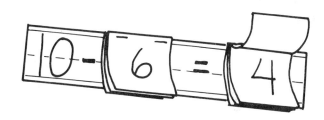

Number Books

Choose a number and write it on a sentence strip. Draw sets that show that number on blank cards. Attach the pile of cards to the sentence strip.

Other Ideas . . .

- Weather books
- Animal books
- Foods for breakfast
- Plant growth
- Nursery rhyme books

Shopping Lists

A shopping list is a time-saving, organizational tool that can help children define their learning goals, plan ahead, and organize their ideas.

Materials:
- paper cut in various sizes
- pencils, crayons, markers

Directions:
Using different sizes of paper, students write shopping lists to organize their ideas. Younger children can draw their lists.

When Nature Gets Upset
Be prepared when a disaster comes your way. Make a shopping list of what you might need.

Buying Balanced Meals
Go grocery shopping for your family. Plan a menu and make the shopping list.

Earthquake Preparedness
1. Water
2. radio
3. flashlight
4. batteries
5. first aid kit
6. wrench
7. sleeping bag
8. tent
9. food

First Aid Kit

Buy
1. watermelon
2. hot dogs
3. buns
4. carrots
5. celery
6. juice
7. bananas
8. pet food
9. milk

Pet food

Milk

Special Jobs

Doing a special job could require a list. Choose a project you might do at home. Write a list of what you will need to complete your project. Be prepared!

Planting a Garden

Research and write what you need to buy for planting a vegetable garden.

Science Exploration

Investigate a specific topic. Plan a science experiment and list what will be needed to explore this area.

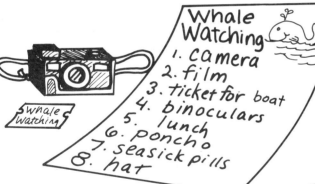

History Lists

Select a period in history. Make a shopping list of what people would need to buy for school based on the availability of goods at that time.

Room Makeover

Make a list of what you would need to decorate your dream bedroom or dream classroom.

Other Ideas . . .

- Lewis and Clark's list
- Admiral Byrd's list
- Space travel
- Supplies for a shut-in
- Food for a zoo

Storyboards

Storyboards are great tools for organizing stories, plays, videos, and even field trips. They can also be used to check recall and comprehension.

Materials:
- pencils, crayons, markers
- storyboard, p. 96

Directions:
Make copies of the storyboard pattern on p. 96. Instruct students to number the frames, illustrate, and label the content in sequence.

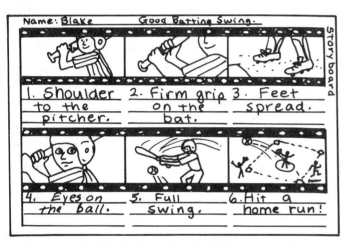

Name: Blake Good Batting Swing.
1. Shoulder to the pitcher. 2. Firm grip on the bat. 3. Feet spread.
4. Eyes on the ball. 5. Full swing. 6. Hit a home run!

Kid Vids
Plan a commercial you want to tape. Use storyboards to show what happens in your commercial.

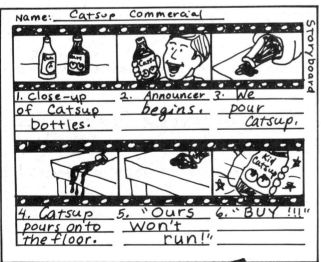

Name: Catsup Commercial
1. Close-up of Catsup bottles. 2. Announcer begins. 3. We pour Catsup.
4. Catsup pours onto the floor. 5. "Ours won't run!" 6. "BUY !!!"

Plays
Choose a fairy tale to make into a play. Make a storyboard to organize your play.

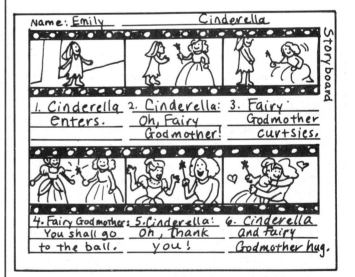

Name: Emily Cinderella
1. Cinderella enters. 2. Cinderella: Oh, Fairy Godmother! 3. Fairy Godmother curtsies.
4. Fairy Godmother: You shall go to the ball. 5. Cinderella: Oh, Thank you! 6. Cinderella and Fairy Godmother hug.

Math

Use a storyboard to demonstrate the steps of a mathematical procedure.

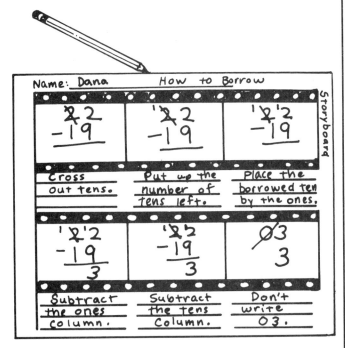

Science Assessment

Plan a science experiment. Use a storyboard to illustrate the procedure, results and conclusion of your experiment.

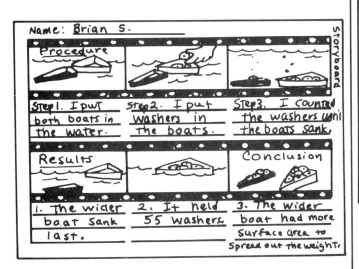

Fantasy Field Trip

Dream up the best school field trip you can imagine. Plan out what will happen, first to last. Illustrate the events on a storyboard.

Life Cycles

Use a storyboard to show the sequence in the growth and development of a reptile, a mammal, or a bird.

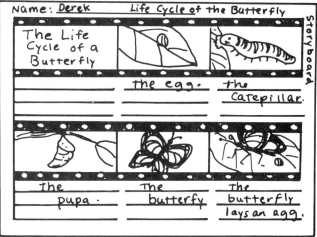

Other Ideas . . .

- Highlights of the school year
- Metamorphosis
- Santa's whole year in twelve panels

Time Lines

Time lines can be used to retrace historical events, record family history, establish future goals, and reminisce past events. It provides opportunity for building community within the class and acquiring knowledge of significant events in our history.

Materials:

- sheets of construction paper
- rolls of paper (optional)
- pencils
- crayons, markers
- colored paper
- glue
- scissors

Directions:

Roll out a strip of paper or glue sheets of paper together to make a long sheet. Have students select a topic to be recorded on the time line. Direct students to record and illustrate important topical events in chronological order. Remind students that time lines use equal increments of time as benchmark measures and show events placed on the line in relation to the benchmarks.

Retelling

Use a time line to retell a story in sequence.

My Life

Record significant events in your life on a time line and illustrate with sketches or photos.

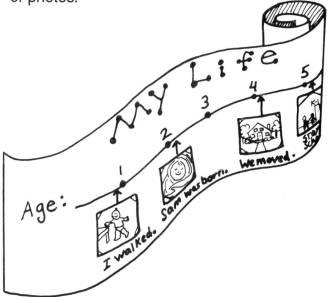

Rock Layers

Use a time line to show how rock layers are formed over millions of years.

Goals for the Future

Select personal goals, family goals, school goals, or goals for the country. Plan a time line for the next three years. Put your goals on the time line to show when you hope you will reach the goal.

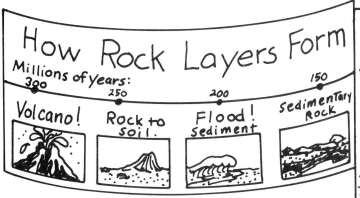

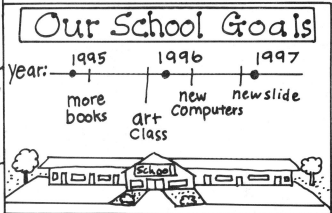

Community History

Choose an event in your community's history. Research the event and show what happened on a time line. Present your time line to the class.

Healthy Living

Develop a time line of your physical fitness activities for the week.

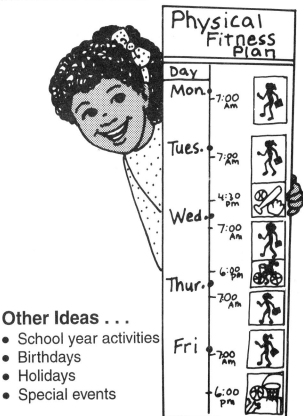

Other Ideas . . .

- School year activities
- Birthdays
- Holidays
- Special events

Travel Guides

Travel guides are fun, motivating, and handy for students to use as they communicate their knowledge. Guides can help students summarize and synthesize important concepts they have learned.

Materials:
- blank paper, 9" x 12" or 12" x 18"
- pencils, crayons, markers
- atlas
- encyclopedias
- maps
- sample travel guides

Directions:
Have students fold a sheet of paper into thirds to create a travel guide. They can design the guide to advertise or display a theme they have been exploring.

Travel Through Time
Design a travel guide to take you back to a particular time in history.

A Safe Vacation
Make a travel pamphlet that shares advice for having a safe vacation.

Endangered Species

Design a pamphlet to persuade people to join a club for saving an endangered species. Include when and where your club will meet and club activities in which members will participate.

Vacation Highlights

Design a travel guide about a family vacation. Include where you would like go and what you might do.

School Tour

Make a tour guide pamphlet for a new student at your school. Include answers to questions new students might ask.

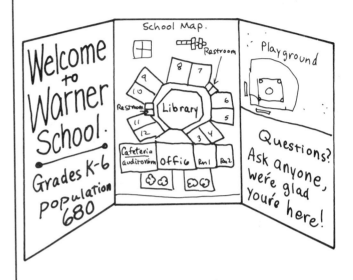

City Tour

Make a travel pamphlet highlighting the most important places in your community. Describe each location and its value to your community.

Other Ideas . . .

- Touring national forests
- Famous tour sites
- Famous stadiums
- Tips for traveling with pets

Tri-Fold Boards

Ease young students into book reporting and presentations by using tri-fold boards that incorporate art, language skills, and content.

Materials:
- colored fabric tape
- hot glue gun or two-sided tape
- articles to be mounted
- heavy cardboard, foam core, or heavy tagboard

Directions:
Instruct students to measure and cut three panels from heavy cardboard or other stable material. Have them decorate and tape boards together with fabric tape. Help them mount graphics with double-sided tape or hot glue.

Science Project
Make a board that explains a science project or experiment. Display the project in front of the tri-fold.

Domino Directions
Mount domino or pattern block pattern cards on one side of your board. Give your partner, sitting on the other side of the board, oral directions on how to complete a pattern card. Challenge your partner to follow your directions without looking.

Social Studies

Research a learning center to teach your friends about an event in history. Use the tri-fold board to display your information.

Language Arts

Gather a cooperative group to choose three characters from a book. Work together to design a character's body on each board panel, making a hole for your face to fit through. Have the whole group get "in character" by making a presentation from behind the tri-fold.

Science

Write and display an animal report that includes a map of the animal's native region, drawings of its habitat, descriptions of its eating and sleeping habits, illustrations of its life cycle, and a list of interesting facts.

Other Ideas . . .

- Study carrels
- Back stage or scenery for plays
- Instruction boards for learning centers
- Grading instruction center for students
- Traveling art fair
- Puppet stage

T-Shirts

Decorated T-shirts are both fun and functional. There are benefits in using this medium for language arts, math, team building, field trips, or social studies.

Materials:
- markers
- old or new T-shirts
- puff paints or acrylics
- cardboard shirt forms
- masking tape
- fabric remnants, buttons
- glue

Directions:
Instruct students to place the cardboard inside their T-shirt, pulling the shirt tight to tape it to the cardboard. Have them use paints, markers, buttons, and fabric remnants to decorate the T-shirt for the activity.

Math Uniform
Make a shirt to wear during math class. Share your facts progress by writing mastered facts on your shirt. Add facts to your shirt as you learn more.

Classroom Shirt
Keep a record of special days and field trips. Wear your shirt on the day of the field trip or special event. Have a friend take notes or write information on your shirt.

History T-Shirt

Use your shirt to design a costume for an important person in America's history. Tell two friends about the person you chose to honor.

Inventor T-Shirts

Design a T-shirt illustrating a real or original invention. Become the inventor and tell everyone about your life and invention.

Noun Shirt

Make a list of nouns with your cooperative group. Write the lists on one another's shirt.

Autographs

On the last day of school have everyone sign your T-shirt. Decorate around the names to show what you liked about school this year.

Other Ideas . . .

- Gift wrapping yourself for Mother's or Father's Day
- Hall pass
- Adding buttons for counting

T. V. Games

Adapt television game shows into classroom games to review curriculum or give new information. Games are motivating and easy to make.

Materials:
- flash cards
- toys, play money
- chalkboard, chalk
- writing paper
- pens, markers, pencils, crayons
- food items
- prizes
- chairs
- pattern, p. 95

Directions:
Select a TV game and curricular topic. Have students design new rules for the game show making flash cards or props they need. Challenge students to research the questions and answers to the game.

Jr. Jeopardy®
Write answers to questions in a given subject. Invite a host to read the answers, and your classmates to raise their hands to provide a question that fits each answer.

Spin The Wheel of Fortune®
Make the spinner on p. 95. Choose a phrase, quote, person, or event from a given topic, and write it as a "hangman" message on the board. Have players take turns spinning the spinner. After each spin, players earn the spun points if they can guess a letter in the puzzle. The player who solves the puzzle is the winner for that round and gets the points he or she has collected from the spins.

Which Price Is Right?

Invent your own version of The Price Is Right®. Draw and display various items with price tags and make prizes. Have your friends play pricing games to win a prize.

Hip Hoppin' Hollywood Squares®

Play Hollywood Squares®. Write questions about math and science subjects. Choose a host, two players, and nine "squares" to represent a tic-tac-toe board.

$300 Pyramid Plus

Write lists of words to describe several history categories such as "What King George Might Say" or "Things Used for Gold Mining in the 1800s". Choose two players—one to read, and one to play. The reader reads a word list from one category. The player has sixty seconds to guess the name of the category being described. If the player names the category before the time is up, he or she receives $100.00 in play money. The players change positions and play again with another word list. The first player to earn $300.00 wins.

Other Ideas . . .

- Pass Word®
- To Tell the Truth®
- Friendly Family Feud®

Wallets

Wallets may be used as a review, a fact finder, or as a means of interaction between students.

Materials:
- construction paper, 9" x 12"
- stapler
- pencils, crayons
- 3" x 5" cards

Directions:
Have students fold the paper in half lengthwise, then into thirds. Help them secure the folds with staples. Invite students to decorate the wallet, and make interior props for each activity.

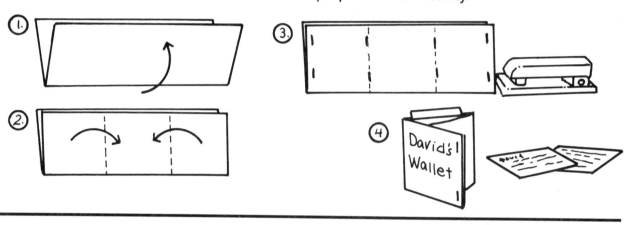

Money Math
Make and cut out coins and paper money from 3" x 5" cards. Place an undisclosed amount of money in your wallet and give it to a partner. Ask your partner to count the money.

Community Helpers
Draw or write facts about a community helper on 3" x 5" cards. Place them in your wallet. Choose a partner, trade wallets, and guess each other's occupations.

Science

Choose a science topic. List facts with illustrations on 3" x 5" cards. Make an ID card stating your science title, such as "Reptile Expert" or "Future Scientist". Carry your ID card in your wallet. Tell a classmate about your science job.

Characters from Literature

Use cards to write or draw facts about a character from literature. Label the wallet with the character's name.

Word Families

Make flash cards for three word families such as *-it, -ther,* or *-ology.* Store the flash cards in your wallet. Practice reading and spelling the word cards during your free time.

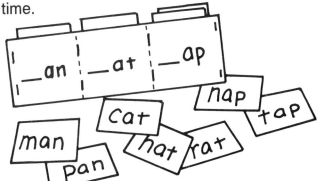

Lost and Found

Write or draw information about yourself on cards without using your name. "Lose" the wallet in the classroom. The finder uses the cards to identify you.

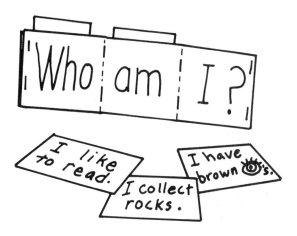

Name Puzzle

Write your name on 3" x 5" cards and cut the letters apart. Place the pieces in your wallet. "Lose" the wallet somewhere in your classroom. Find someone's "lost" wallet, put the name together and return the wallet to the owner.

Other Ideas . . .

- Color words
- Number words
- Famous scientists
- Laminated math flash card holder
- Parts of speech
- Message carrier

Wordless Books

To encourage creativity and freedom of expression, wordless books make great motivators. Wordless books allow students to write or retell stories without being inhibited by spelling, grammar, or punctuation.

Materials:
- blank paper
- pencils, crayons, markers, paints
- books
- poems, short stories
- hole punch
- yarn
- binding machine (optional)
- plastic bags (optional)

Directions:
Choose a subject area, a literature selection to rewrite, or a topic for a nonfiction report. Have students illustrate scenes on each page, design a cover, and write a title for each activity. Help students bind the book with yarn or a machine. Have students protect pages by sealing them in plastic bags.

Story Recall
Retell a story in pictures. Include details and follow the story's sequence.

Science
Select a science topic. Illustrate the topic in the wordless book. Use the book to give an oral science presentation.

Math

Brainstorm places where people spend money. Choose one place and make a book about a character who spends all his money.

Communities

Design a book that compares your community with others throughout the state or country.

Movies on a Bookshelf

Recreate your favorite movie by making a wordless book that retells the story.

My Life

Make a wordless book that tells your life story. Continue the story to tell your future.

Other Ideas . . .
- Cartoons
- Family
- Friendship

Cereal Box Pattern

Write or draw on the sides of the box pattern. Cut out the pattern. Fold on the dotted lines. Glue the sides together.

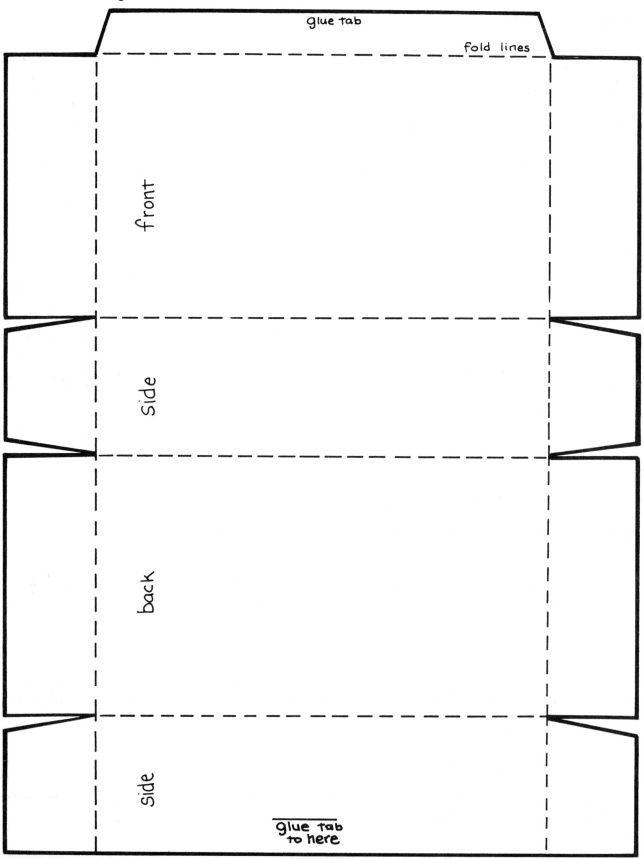

MORE Alternative to Worksheets   Creative Teaching Press

Coding Patterns

When writing a message in code, use a slash (/) between words.

1. Position Code

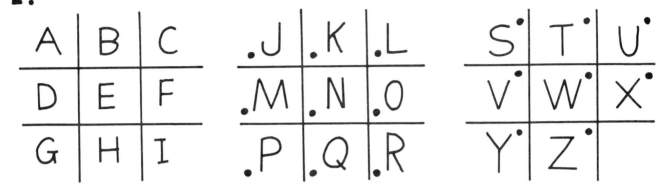

2. Braille Alphabet

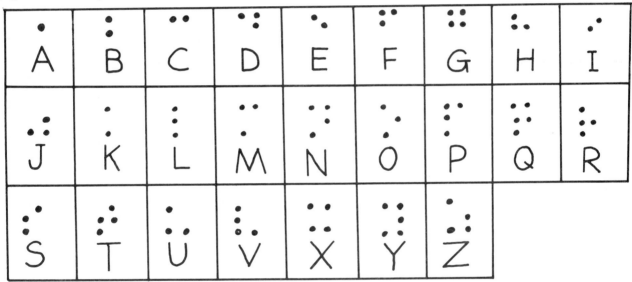

3. Pictograph Code

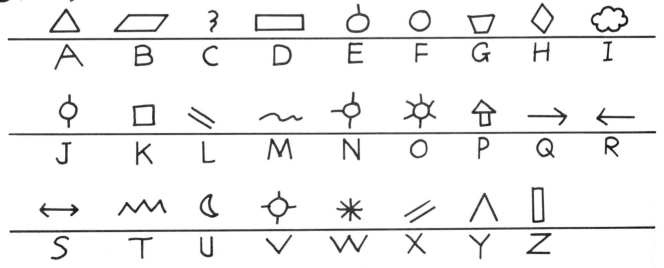

Eyeglasses Pattern

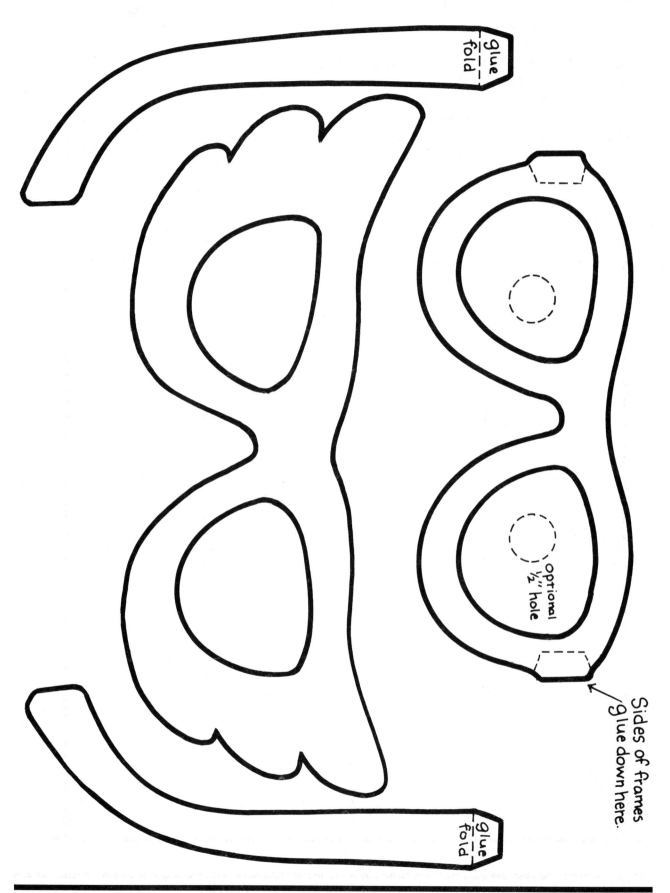

glue
fold

glue
fold

optional
½" hole

Sides of frames
glue down here.

MORE Alternative to Worksheets

Creative Teaching Press

Fact Catchers

1. Fold square into fourths. Open.
2. Fold A points corner to center to form a smaller square.
3. Flip over and fold B points corner to center forming an even smaller square.
4. Eight right triangles should be showing. The triangles are connected in pairs making four flaps. Write four questions or clues on top of the flaps. Pull open the flaps and write the answers on the underside of each flap.
5. Fold the small square in half to reveal four square pockets for fingers. Number the finger pockets one through four.

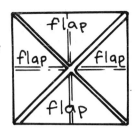

View #2

View #3

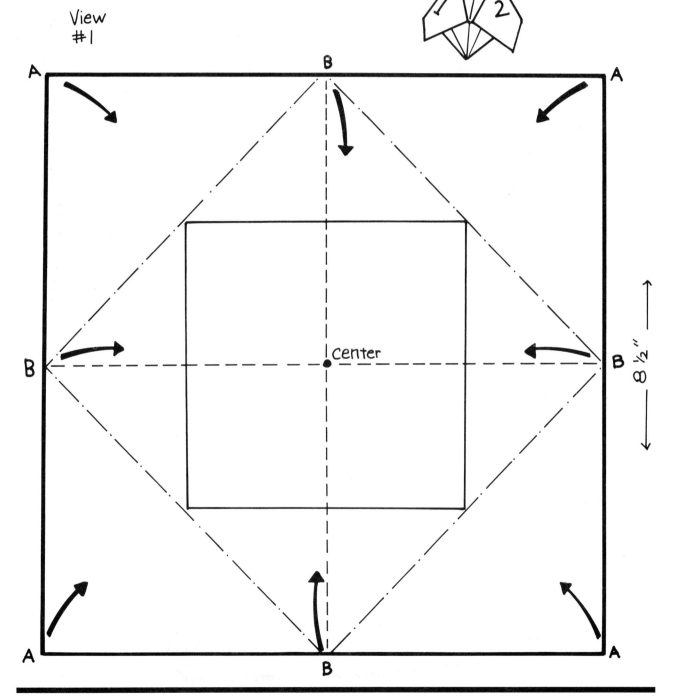

View #1

Flip-Flip Book

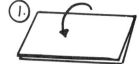

1. Fold each 18" x 18" sheet of paper and unfold to make four 9" squares for each sheet.

2. Lay the three 18" x 18" sheets of paper in a pile.

3. Cut the pile from the left edges to the center along the folds. **Make sure to stop cutting at the center of the sheets.**

4. Fold the top left square over to the right side of the stack.Then fold the two squares from the top right downward, moving in a clockwise direction.

5. After the first two folds are made, tape the bottom left square of the top layer of paper to the top left square of the second layer.

6. Once you have taped the first two layers together continue to fold the small squares clockwise in the direction of left, up, right, and down. **Be careful to keep the book in the same position on your desk, never rotating the layers.**

7. Once you come to the third layer, tape the bottom left square of the second layer of paper to the top left square of the third layer.

8. Without rotating the book, continue to fold clockwise until all the small squares are in one pile.

9. Use the movable small square on the outside for a cover. Open the book and number the inside of the cover #1 and the small square to the right #2. Unfold the book once more and place #3 on the top right square. Do not number the top left square but unfold down and number the revealed page #4. Continue unfolding and numbering revealed pages in a counter clockwise direction to 12.

10. Write text and illustrations on the twelve numbered squares. Decorate the cover and make a large 18" x 18" illustration at the end of the book. **The book pages will be in order if the book is not rotated. Keep the book in one position on your desk.**

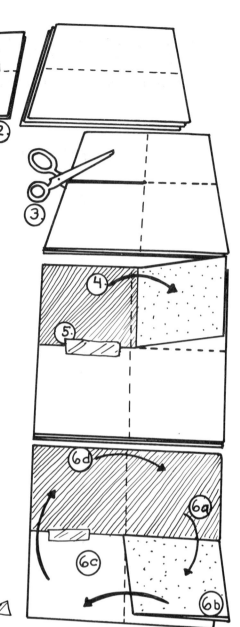

MORE Alternative to Worksheets   Creative Teaching Press

Light Switch Pattern

Decorate the light switch cover. Cut out the pattern. Tape the light switch cover in place.

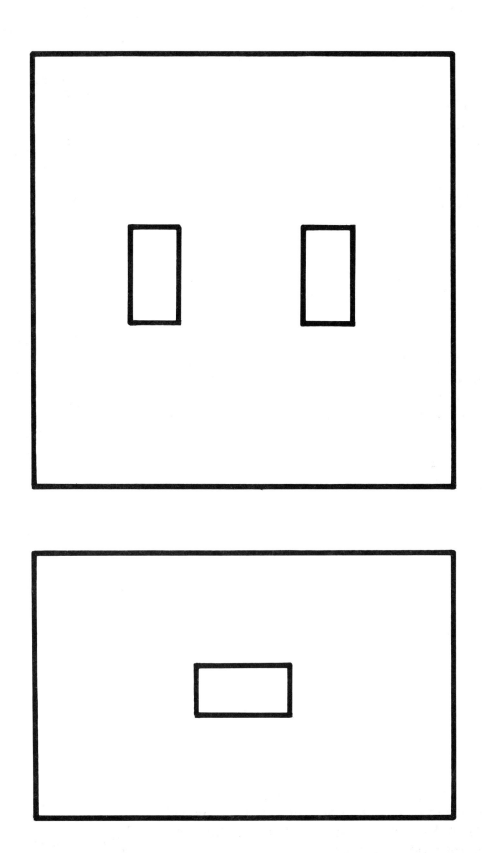

Paper Doll Pattern

MORE Alternative to Worksheets Creative Teaching Press

Pencil Holder Pattern

Write or draw on the sides of the pencil holder pattern. Cut out the pattern. Fold on the dotted lines. Tape or glue the sides together. Tape the pencil holder to the index card to make a bottom. Tape the index card and pencil holder to your desk.

Pinwheel Pattern

Cut out pattern. Cut along lines to end points. Fold corners one through four to center point and attach with a brad.

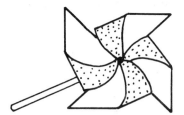

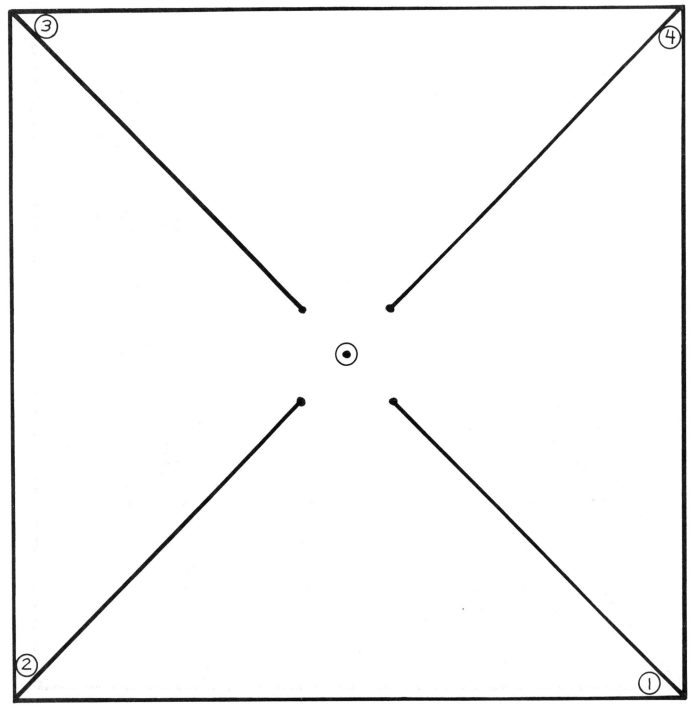

MORE Alternative to Worksheets Creative Teaching Press

Spinner Pattern

Attach a brad in the center of the spinner. Put a paper clip around the spinner.

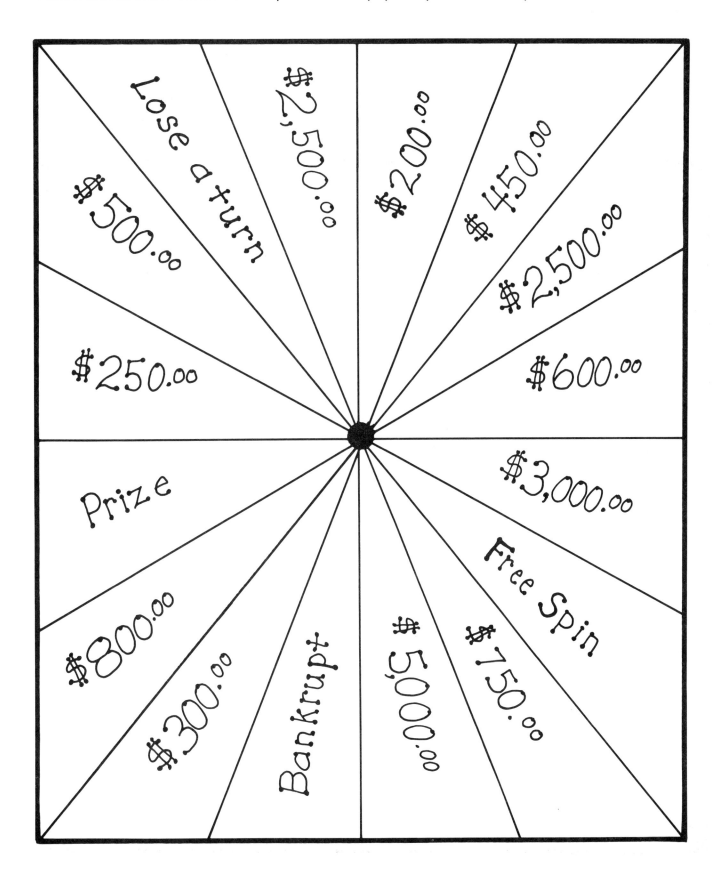

Storyboard

MORE Alternative to Worksheets Creative Teaching Press